Mind, Decentralized

MIND, DECENTRALIZED

BECOMING MASTERLESS

Rob Brinded

Edited by Mel Shilling and Niko Laamanen

KONSENSUS NETWORK

Edited by Mel Shilling and Niko Laamanen
Cover design and typesetting by Konsensus Network
Rob's photo on page 94 — Hormos Carls @tatsatoshi
Illustrations not otherwise marked — *Rob Brinded*.
ISBN 978-9916-723-34-0 Hardcover
978-9916-723-35-7 Paperback
978-9916-723-36-4 E-book
KONSENSUS NETWORK https://konsensus.network

Contents

To Sylvia, Lima & Bo

for your love and showing me what I need to work on.

Foreword

"What's the best sex you've ever had?"

Imagine that being the question that changed your life's work!

And no, it didn't come from a sleazy porn director in the basement of a dingy house directed towards the person sitting on the casting couch. It was asked by Rob Brinded at Chelsea FC's state-of-the-art Sports and Injury Prevention Medical facility and directed at one of the best Football players in the world at that time.

Why did Rob ask that question? What did it reveal to him, and how did that lead to him quitting his 'perfect life'?

Even before the athlete answered, Rob knew he had unlocked an incredibly important discovery. A discovery that would change the trajectory of his life. One that would trigger him to walk away from a high-paying job, get dumped by his girlfriend, and be shunned by his professional peers while facing the inner demons and self-torture of disappointment.

During this time, Rob forged a new mindset, armed himself with the tools to cure himself, and extended that healing touch to anyone who had the fortune of interacting with him.

Like many of my new friends, I first met Rob on Twitter. He approached me after I had been the featured guest on *The Bitcoin Standard Podcast.* My discussion with host Saifedean Ammous centred around the intricacies of the current education system and the benefits of homeschooling. Rob had been particularly intrigued by my insights about teaching versus learning and how our education system is designed to mould kids rather than nurture and inspire them. But what truly piqued Rob's curiosity was what I didn't say. Throughout the podcast conversation, he wanted to ask about certain nuances, the pauses. Because, well, that's the way Rob's mind works now!

Over the next few months, Rob and I stayed in contact and eventually had the pleasure of meeting each other in Madeira when we received an invitation to assemble with other bitcoiners to meet the President, as he and his cabinet wanted to learn more about bitcoin and the opportunities it might bring to their island.

Extended, in-person conversations with Rob about his work are truly fascinating. During our first meet-up, I found myself open to everything he shared. Some people he has encountered have brushed him off as a 'Guru' or too 'Woo-Woo' and thought his ideas were too far out there. The irony here is that their feelings are triggered by the very conditioning and programming that these people have been subjected to and have been running from their whole lives. As Rob would explain, the only way to step off the hamster wheel is to realise you are on it in the first place. Most people don't and will forever be trapped, running the same self-deprecating programmes for their whole lives.

I was so captivated by Rob's ideas that I booked him for a few sessions (paid in bitcoin) to learn more about his work and, of course, myself. My goal was to understand why I thought the way I thought and why I acted the way I acted under certain stressors. With a spirit of open exploration, we embarked on a journey through my past, present and future, engaging in candid conversations that flowed effortlessly. Rob's guidance helped me decipher the programs I had been running in my head (my OS system) and how to close them down. I can best surmise it with the analogy of 'force-quitting' a program on your computer when you get the 'spinning beach ball of death'.

Once you do this simple visualisation exercise, a remarkable transformation occurs — you feel lighter and think clearer. Like our minds, our bodies can react in the most incredible ways. Lifelong ailments, aches, or pains can feel instantly better and even disappear completely.

Rob's conviction in his work is not from blind luck; it's rooted in decades of deep introspection mixed with theoretical and practical study — and, importantly, from results. The outcomes Rob has seen and shared in this book are beyond remarkable and worth everyone's attention. As you journey through these pages and into this rabbit hole, remember to note what emotions are triggered within YOU carefully. Because that, dear reader, is your personal hamster wheel. Those triggered emotions have been programmed into your OS since you were born, and those programs are what hold you back mentally and physically from being your best self and living a happier and freer life.

So, sit back and enjoy the ride. Welcome to the rabbit hole of decentralising your mind!

Daniel Prince

Host of The Once Bitten Podcast and Author of *Choose Life*
Block Height 800,608 — SW France

Preface

Writing this book made me acutely aware of my conditioning around *able* and *unable*. This book became my teacher. I realised that I started this book off as a way to feel more able — to be recognised by others as capable, intelligent and smart. I knew this because when I told people about this project, I got a buzz of excitement not from the work of writing but from how people perceived me as an "author." This slowly took hold of me. Writing became hard. I was blocked and started to dread the idea of writing further.

It was a wonderful opportunity to discover this hamster wheel I was on that I hadn't seen for 50 years. I observed the thought pop in my head that "I should be writing the book," and then the guilt and shame that followed. I watched and looked deeper at these emotions, following the smoke until I could see the flames.

It took two months of observing, the longest a behaviour had stayed around for me. As time passed, I could see the behaviour becoming increasingly panicked, but I didn't jump back on the hamster wheel. I just observed.

Then, one day, I saw the unable and able pattern on my balcony. It was everywhere, and it shocked me. I immediately felt immense grief and sadness. This was and is, for most, a behaviour conditioned from a very early age. It has driven me in every aspect of my life. Unpacking this discovery was one of the greatest reliefs of my life.

As if now magnetically drawn to being able, I walked calmly into my office that day and finished the book. The way to be more able is not in striving but in watching how unable we truly are, and in seeing it, we dissolve it.

As Snoop Dogg so eloquently said in a speech, “I would like to thank me for being me” and for spending the last 30 years looking for why I was so deeply insecure and not content and why I had so much pain in my body.

Throughout my career, I have always focused on results for myself and my clients. I was compulsively driven to be as able as possible, bringing with it the deepest usableness. However, from this journey, I have discovered the greatest riches I now share as a guide for others to become like me: masterless through a decentralised mind.

The significance of my logo lies in its depiction of the ronin or warrior, symbolising the internal struggle we all must face to become masterless. To become truly masterless, one must first embrace decentralised money — bitcoin. In doing so, we can reject government control and central bank digital currencies, which enable control of our spending habits and imposition of fines if we do not obey their commands. Becoming masterless also requires decentralised health. For instance, if you do not want to take the next experimental drug that is coming, you must have decentralised your approach to your wellness so that you do not succumb to the doctor’s authority or the pharmaceutical industry. You can make informed choices aligned with your values. Finally and critically, we must cultivate and fortify our decentralised mind to free us from the incessant hamster wheel and experience lasting peace.

With no external authority controlling us, especially not our minds, we are empowered to live life on our own terms. Only then can we become masterless.

Layers of Becoming Masterless

Imagine this figure represents the layers of becoming masterless. The bottom layer symbolised the soil. Akin to the foundational layer of bitcoin, it is slow and difficult to change. This is where Meditation OS and self-observation reside. They allow us to observe our conditioning and to see our internal prison. Through this awareness, we can revolutionise the known within our minds.

Moving up to the next layer, which is smaller, we encounter lightning meditation. Here, we find the activity monitor, helping us identify and switch off things that drain our systems.

At the top and smallest portion of the triad lies exercise, food, water, and enjoyment of your way of life. Outside, we see nature's code, electrical ones and zeros as in *The Matrix*. For example, the colour yellow[1] signifies the sun, emphasising the need to embrace natural light. Just as plants and animals do, we need to be energised by that life force emanating from the sun's energy.

These three essential elements show the path to becoming masterless and cultivating a decentralised mind. Navigating this triad allows us to experience peace and harmony within our bodies, maintain good health, and relish life's pleasures while maximising our journey while we relish our heaven on earth. And at the core of all three rests truth.

[1] See the back cover of the book for a colour version of the logo

I

The Mind Decentralised

On a warm summer's afternoon in 1998 at the Chelsea Football Club training ground, I was in my strength and conditioning gym when an "aha" moment shook me off of my 'central mind' cliff — the fragile intellectual mountain's edge where I had been teetering for the past year. There, I discovered my first real 'red pill' that transported me down a spiritual rabbit hole.

And with that, my way of looking at the body as a collection of separate parts, like a physical robot, unintelligent and fully understood by our superior intellect, was obliterated. Instead, I embarked on a quest to comprehend how the mind, its emotions, and fundamental consciousness affected the body and its environment. It is a journey I am still walking today.

Before I explain further, here is some background for this fateful day.

From the outside, I had the perfect life. One of the highest-paid strength and conditioning experts in Europe, I had developed my own Injury Prevention Centre in Chelsea FC, which was tasked with analysing players and working out which players had a higher risk of injury. I had created a simple 'traffic light' evaluation protocol to assess risk. I would argue that the system was advanced for its time and is still advanced now. Drawing on the mystery-solving techniques learned from my childhood hero, Sherlock Holmes, I regarded each athlete's body as a unique puzzle to be solved. Unlocking the secrets to their bodies produced my trademark product — peak athletic performances.

The playing squad at the time was worth over £250 million, so there was an incentive to keep those players available to José Mourinho, the charismatic Portuguese manager. Mourinho put huge pressure on the medical team to get players to recover as fast as possible. At the time, we had the best medical team performance for injury recoveries in Europe.

In my personal life, I had a beautiful girlfriend and a little house in the countryside where I could glimpse deer or foxes throughout the day on the rare moments when I wasn't working. While I looked healthy from the outside, I'd started losing energy, had constant back pain, and lived on five to six cups of coffee daily. I still remember the polystyrene cups I would nibble to ensure no one else drank them.

Looking back now, I was on a slippery slope to metabolic syndrome and fatigue. I was doing my best and kept my mask on tight so people thought I had my shit together.

I felt completely empty. I was wracked with insecurity and easily hurt emotionally at work. I worked in an excessively male-dominant and aggressive environment that made me uncomfortable. Of course, I realise now that the deeply competitive, on-field, athletic culture carried over to all aspects of club management. I was naive and trusted everyone, but I learned the hard way that 'trust' was perceived as weak. Someone was always looking to take advantage of my work or put it down. One story encapsulates this well.

When I arrived at the club, I met a male masseur who liked to do a bit of basic training with the athletes on the side. From the moment I arrived, he turned on me, making snide comments behind my back and sometimes to my face. One time, I brought a star player to his room who had just received treatment on the medical table. As I relayed what the physiotherapist had told me, the masseur slammed the door in my face. This hurt and confused me, and it kept me up at night. Dr. Fraser helped me with the situation and stood up for me, and I thank him for that. The situation escalated. When the masseur learned that the manager had invited me to join pre-season training due to my effective work and the players' request, the masseur became angry and swore loudly. I then witnessed him crumble from within over the next few days. Eventually, he was hospitalised while on tour in Italy. The masseur said it was because he'd eaten a monkey while trekking in the jungle the month before. But I know it was because I triggered something so deep inside of him it made him sick.

I now understand that it wasn't 'me,' but his wounds I triggered. His envy and jealousy made him sick, psychically and physically. I also realised that my reaction to his behaviour was my 'stuff,' my issues. And like the masseur, my issues were slowly poisoning me.

Fundamentally, I believed that if I worked for one of the most famous sports teams in the world, I would have achieved my ambitions, and I would have won this game of life. But I was far from winning. I was lost and deeply unhappy.

For years, I had been studying in my own time with Paul Chek, a holistic health coach from San Diego. His foundational work was body-centric, focusing on functional training for athletes. As I dug into his work, I began learning about Eastern practices, unfamiliar to most people I worked with. I studied Tai Chi, Qigong, Reiki, and various spiritual healing modalities. I devoured spiritual books to understand myself better and heal myself internally. These explorations revealed the world beyond the physical, and I began understanding the importance of non-physical health. I was desperate to alleviate my physical, mental, and emotional pain.

My schizophrenic work life started to bring me down. I was passionate about delving deeper into the Eastern philosophies in my practice and introducing them to the players. But the medical team were 'based' in science, meaning if there wasn't a research paper on it, you couldn't use it. They were fixed in their centralised, linear-thinking minds.

A storm brewed inside of me. I talked to the players about their feelings more and more and began seeing patterns when a player was stressed that he was more likely to show up in the medical room with pain somewhere in his body. I did more yoga with the players, for instance, with the Dutch football player Arjen Robben. His nature was kind and sympathetic, and he frequently stressed and worried about things around him. He was often injured. So, I prescribed yoga to him to stimulate his parasympathetic nervous system and to balance him out. I did Tai Chi and Qigong exercises with Gianfranco Zola, who took to it like a duck to water. On the sly, I even started doing Reiki and energy work on players in their own time.

Years later, I met a UK football physiotherapist in Barcelona and mentioned my work over twenty years ago. He couldn't believe I had introduced this type of work to the players so long ago and told me they were integrating these approaches now. That comment struck me and brought up anger that I hadn't stood by my guns and should have been prouder of my work. I observed my own reaction, and later in life, I have come to understand that self-observation is key to undoing internal knots. (More on this later in the book.)

This perfect storm was always going to break at some point. And it happened on this fateful day in my gym. I will be forever appreciative of the penetrating bolt of insight.

The moment came when I was surrounded by my medical team: a podiatrist, a chiropractor, a physiotherapist, and a doctor. I was setting up for one of my posturology assessments. Posturology is a method of looking at all the different types of receptors that tell the body where to position itself. Receptors include the eyes, the skin of the feet, or even scars, short leg syndrome, or a pre-bite in the teeth. When receptors receive faulty information, the body can position itself incorrectly. Or, to find the best position possible, the body puts itself out of perfect balance.

The test involves two highly sensitive weighing machines to measure a weight shift imbalance. The athlete places one foot on each scale, with a plumb line in front of the athlete, down the middle. A gridded screen in the background facilitates informative before and after photos for studying later. I also videotaped the whole assessment.

The first athlete, the best in the world in his position, walked in, ready for further instruction. I had my clipboard with my assessment protocol, poised to record measurements. As the athlete stood on the two scales, I looked down and noted a reading of 8 kg heavier on the right leg. Now, 8 kg is momentous, and it shocked everyone. I turned to look at the other team members, who were all surprised. Going by his skill set, the chiropractor said, "This is probably his Atlas, coming from the neck." The podiatrist said, "Oh, this is probably a short leg." The doctor stood there with his syringe, looking at where to inject him. Joke.

I listened to them and commenced my assessment. But something deep inside said: "Wait... Rob, you need to see if there's an emotional input!"

My secret journey came to a head right then. The spiritual realm that I'd been studying clamoured to escape. For me to open my mouth in front of the medical team and to say this was a massive moment. One I'll never forget. I was incredibly nervous. I hesitated for a second, then blurted:

"What's the best sex you've ever had?"

I looked into his eyes; they looked up to the left and sort of flicked backwards and forward like he was searching folders in his memory. I didn't care what he answered. I just kept glancing at the scales out of the corner of my eye. As he shared the girl's nationality with a smile — I remember this moment perfectly — I looked at the perfectly balanced scales. The 8 kg discrepancy was completely gone. He was bang on the button balanced!

Now, with all my posturology training and the thousands of hours of training spent with the best in the world in their respective fields, I could never have gotten this athlete balanced so quickly and effectively without ever touching him. I was absolutely shocked.

I turned to look at the medical staff and asked, "Did you see that?" The doctor's eyes glazed over. I now recognise that look in his eyes as cognitive dissonance, an inability to comprehend the magnitude of what just happened. It simply did not fit with his model of reality. It was the slightest crack of light into his centralised control of knowledge of the body. If a thought could significantly disrupt the body, it would mean that the model underpinning physiology as purely anatomy and machine parts was fundamentally incorrect. He didn't want to acknowledge that.

To see if I was correct, I then asked the player to recall, without saying aloud, the worst moment of his life. This time, he accessed the thought quickly, like retrieving a memory file on his mind computer. He said, "I remember." A palpable sense inside my body felt his energy drop. I looked at the scales. He was nine kilos heavier on one leg. With one memory, he had moved even further into imbalance.

What just happened?

The first thought 'strengthened' his balance, strengthened his body. The second thought — the painful, difficult thought — put his body out of balance, weakening it. I now know this. One strengthened him, and one weakened him, like a one and a zero code, on or off.

I didn't try to convince the rest of the team; I was in an alternative reality to them. I must admit that I was so insecure and lacking confidence in my intellect that I didn't feel I could explain it. I knew that when I opened my mouth and tried to explain energy, my words would spill out in a confused jumble.

That evening, as I walked home to my house nearby in Cobham, I clearly recall stepping through the grass and looking down at my feet, asking myself, "What happened there?"

I knew in my deepest knowing that I had discovered something profound. Something incredible had happened, and I needed to find out what it was. How on Earth could I access it so I could help people? This was the holy grail for performance: instant results without touch. But how could I master this?

This was the start of my journey from a centralised understanding of the body to a decentralised one, where everything is connected via energy and consciousness.

2

Un-Controlling

To understand the concept of a centralised mind, we must first delve into the history of humankind and explore significant shifts in power structures. Through time, these shifts marked a transition from a centralised control structure to a decentralised one. I like to call this 'un-controlling,' as they happened accidentally, without the mind moulding the outcome. They took place organically as a natural progression of societal evolution.

These seismic shifts in society coincided with discoveries and inventions that enabled humans to grow more efficiently, survive and thrive.

The discovery of fire was a massive moment when humans discovered a way to keep themselves warm, ward off predators, and cook food. Fire was also used to hunt and clear land. Harnessing this discovery catapulted the evolution of humans to where we are today.

Later, advances in weapon technology shaped wars and changed geographical territories. In Rees-Mogg and Davidson's *The Sovereign Individual*, they describe what happens when this technology is shared:

> When key technologies are hoarded, this tends to centralise power. So, the more widely technologies are dispersed, the more power is dispersed. This could be seen with machine guns being widely dispersed after the Second World War, enabling the fall of empires.

We also saw a huge change in society with the invention of the printing press. This innocuous technology disrupted the centralised control of religion. The Church enforced a monopoly on Biblical information and used its power to control and shape the populous. People had to depend on and trust the religious authorities to access the word of God. Total subjugation to authority.

The printing press not only revolutionised education by increasing accessibility to information through books but also disrupted the control of centralised power, distributing it away from the Church. Everyone could have a Bible and make decisions and interpretations for themselves as long as they could read. So, this small-in-size invention sparked unforeseen consequences that disrupted a massive centralised control powerhouse, decentralising information to the people.

An unprecedented move toward greater self-authority.

The next comparable invention, and one I was alive to witness, was the internet. This revolutionary technology continues decentralising information so everyone can access the world's knowledge through their devices. Previously, governments, institutions, and mainstream media outlets tightly controlled the dissemination of information, advancing the state's talking points — and shaping mass opinion via newspapers, radio, and television. To some extent, that remains true, but at least we now have options.

Before the internet, printed books and pamphlets were the only way common people could share their points of view with the population, aside from standing on a soap box in Speakers' Corner in London's Hyde Park and hoping people would stop to listen. However, each individual has a mouthpiece and enjoys access to information once exclusive to the privileged elite. For instance, medical information is now readily available for all, shaking the god complex doctors once held. Medical research, too, is shared faster throughout the world, improving access to medical advances. Light is shining on the Big Pharma-captured medicine industry, slowly disinfecting the corruption festering within the oligarchy. This decentralisation of information has triggered a seismic shift in society.

As technology progresses, the centralised mainstream media becomes more irrelevant. Independent podcasters like Joe Rogan now generate more views than CNN and the BBC combined.

We can argue that this is a good thing. However, as with anything in life, there is a flip side. Good and bad, of course, are relative. We now must slog through an abundance of weaponised disinformation, an info war enabling states and governments to, on a mass scale, shape people's behaviour and programming through their always-on mobile phones.

As @dergigi tweeted: *"Information is free. Attention is not."* Your attention is a prized commodity; the tech is free, and we are the products.

A battle is underway for your attention, and whoever wins this info war will shape and condition humankind.

Information toxicity

Television has always been a distraction tool for people's minds, giving them respite from the mundanity of their lives. The drug of the masses it gradually dulls their minds with each passing day.

The internet has opened the floodgates for knowledge and distraction on a level never seen in history. This online virtual world is where human minds seek pleasure and excitement. But it is an illusion, a mirage. There are no answers to our internal world online. The internet accelerates learning but also unlocks chaos and helplessness.

The pursuit of information is a slippery slope to addiction. As I write, I feel my mind, my attention, drawn to valuable knowledge on Twitter. There, I can scroll to find information that can make me more certain and safe. I need it and feel the urge to check my phone. I am aware of this struggle and watch it at play. My centralised mind tempts me, and I observe the carrot or stick it uses to entice me. Through observing this from a decentralised mind, I dissolve it, leaving me at peace as creativity flows through my fingers.

Ironically, while feeling the centralised mind's pull, I almost posted the above on Twitter. I was nearly lured into the trap. In the words of John Milton, "The mind is its own place and, in itself, can make a Heaven of Hell, a Hell of Heaven."

As is true with the double-edged sword of progress, with the advent of the internet came another brilliant — and as of yet unappreciated — decentralised invention: bitcoin.

Bitcoin

Bitcoin's inventor, Satoshi Nakamoto, set loose the world's first decentralised money — then disappeared. He understood the power of his invention lay in its absence of central control or authority. He did this as a reaction to the bailing out of the banks in the financial crash of 2008. Centralised money managers printed currency out of thin air, diluting the value of people's savings and increasing the wealth gap between the rich and the poor.

We are now witnessing, perhaps, the greatest shift in how the world functions. Transitioning from centralised fiat money to decentralised hard money, bitcoin slowly disrupts and absorbs banks, states, and even the military-industrial war machines.

Authors of the 1990s book *The Sovereign Individual* forecast the discovery of this disruptive and peaceful invention. They understood that the technology was inevitable as the world would become increasingly tyrannical along with fiat currencies collapsing. They predicted that to counter-balance the increase in control, a technology would emerge to diminish that control. They knew that the more the governments sought to control this uncontrollable technology, the more they incentivised people to seek alternatives. The yin to the yang.

> *"...all we can do is by* ***some*** *sly roundabout* ***way*** *introduce something that they can't stop."*
>
> — F.A. Hayek

The Taoists understood the nature and rules of the human mind centuries ago. People have heard of yin and yang but rarely grasp how this applies to every aspect of our lives. The yin and yang rules apply when we play the centralised mind games. As we try to shape our lives one way, we will inevitably energise the opposite. When we act according to our minds to shape the external world, we inevitably sculpt the opposite. We can see it in the creation of bitcoin.

Bitcoin was born out of the unfettered printing of fiat money out of thin air. The excessive abundance of fiat money created financial scarcity for most and overabundance for a select few. The wealth inequality was artificially created. Bitcoin, the first absolutely scarce thing humanity has known, inevitably levels the playing field across space and time. Out of this scarcity, abundance may grace us all.

> *"**Abundance** in money creates scarcity everywhere else, scarcity in money creates **abundance** everywhere else."*
>
> — Jeff Booth

3

The Key to the Prison of the Centralised Mind

My realisation of the flaw in the centralised mind was a gradual one. A gradual understanding until I experienced a deep knowing. It was like taking a lift to different floors until I reached the basement. The journey is ongoing.

I arrived at different floors via different learning experiences. I will share some of the most important ones using stories from my time in football.

Centralised dogma and the way to rehabilitation

Wayne Bridge, a football player for Chelsea FC and the national English football team, smashed and broke his ankle one day in a match. I remember watching, thinking that his recovery would consume much of my future, not to mention months in rehabilitation for him. It was a severe ankle break, and he needed surgery.

I remember the physiotherapists giving him to me and saying, "Look, just humour him and keep him generally fit until we can actually start working the ankle. Then we'll start getting into more specific work in a few months." The head physiotherapist mentioned tissue repair from a physiotherapy book — his bible — and that was that. I agreed and told him I would do as he said.

The first day we met in the gym, Wayne stood cautiously before me, his foot out of its cast. We discussed how he was doing and what he had been up to. Wayne told me how frustrating recovery had been and how itchy his foot was.

I asked him what he could do in terms of movement. He acknowledged very little. I asked if he could sit on the toilet, and he replied yes. I immediately thought, "Well, if he can lower himself onto the toilet and then stand up again, that's a squat. So he can do squats!"

We began his journey with something I knew he could do: squats. I remember specifically asking him to hold onto a bar in a cage so that his central nervous system (CNS) felt calm and safe. The CNS is like a computer system monitoring for any danger or threat.

I had seen studies showing athletes who ran maximally to exhaustion always had carbohydrate stores left in the muscles. So it wasn't running out of fuel that limited performance, but the CNS stopping the body from over-exerting the heart. So, the CNS's perception of an activity is the master. That's why I got Wayne to support himself with the bar. He was carrying even less than his body weight. He did ten reps, and I stopped him to assess how his ankle/CNS responded to this stressor. Fortunately, everything seemed fine. This positive response prompted me to modify his training program to 2 times 10. Next, I removed his hands from the bar. He quickly progressed to three sets of 20 body-weight squats without needing any support. Curious about potential problems, I asked Wayne, "Any issues?" To which he confidently replied, "No!"

Ultimately, we progressed his rehabilitation based on Wayne's unique physical and mental state, not relying on any books to tell me studies done on average individuals. Wayne was a physical specimen and not the average. As such, relying on a central authority to tell me what to do didn't make sense. Yes, you have to respect the anatomy, but the medicalisation of sports and conditioning often hinders performance and is overly cautionary. Having such a central authority thwarts learning: obey the experts and never question. Because the type of people who work in medicine are logical, they typically narrow their focus into specialities, which can make them even more narrow-minded and unaware of human complexity. My approach was to simply observe Wayne's capabilities and efficiently adapt the stressors.

A few months later, the physiotherapist approached me and said, "Rob, you can start doing bodyweight squats with Wayne now." I chuckled privately because we were already beyond that point. By now, Wayne was doing single-leg pistol squats on his 'bad' leg, whereby he would balance on one leg with the other leg in front and lower his hip all the way to the floor. Pistol squats are very difficult for ordinary, healthy people. Medical books prescribe a specific recovery time for tissues, but an intuitive, athlete-led program paces it based on the individual's progress and how they are feeling. As a result, Wayne Bridge recovered in half of the time projected by the medical experts.

Don't get me wrong, it doesn't always work out like that, but you must observe what is in front of you and not blindly follow "the manual" and do what you're told. The confusion I often experience around physiotherapists results from my open mind observing athletes conflicting with the physiotherapists' centrally fixated minds accustomed to working on static outcomes. Also, the athlete's operating system and mind are often fixated on the injury. By incorporating tasks and movements that diverted the mind's attention away from the injury site, I observed a significant improvement in the overall functioning of the patient's body and the reintegration of the injured area.

Getting the mind out of the body

Through trial and error, I realised that my most crucial role in working with athletes was to get their minds out of their bodies. Separating the mind from the body is an effective protective mechanism when injured. Athletes often fixate on their injury and its effect on every aspect of their lives, from job status to identity. More often than not, the injury becomes too protected. The body quickly overcompensates and creates energy leaks, so less force is placed through the joint. This can have devastating long-term effects.

With my conditioning work and any work with the body, I realised the body needs to be given the right position and opportunity to do what it's supposed to do without any danger. Something has gone wrong, and the body craves a bit of guidance to find its way back to harmony. Like a garden, we want to bring it back to balance so that it may look after itself. I have come to understand that the ego likes to think it finds the solutions and is indispensable, but that ego-centric approach ultimately damages everyone involved.

Many factors converged in my life to teach me that lesson. The swashbuckling José Mourinho, the Portuguese coach, was one. He arrived at the Chelsea Football Club with his unique conditioning system and incredible confidence. Mourinho's whole Portuguese team, including Rui Faria, his fitness coach, exuded energy and enthusiasm that lifted everyone around them.

From the start, Mourinho team's general aggressiveness towards the medical team baffled me. Mourinho and his new coaches squashed any attempts by the medical staff to influence the team, especially relating to fitness parameters. At one point, Rui and I discussed the details of how I worked. When he saw what I was doing, that I was just trying to help the athlete regain their body's wisdom, he liked it. Through this, we became good friends. But towards the medical team? Yikes. I now understand why José was the way he was.

Both José and Rui understood the arrogance of the centralised medical mind and how all-important this medical mind thought it was in shaping a team. They knew that you needed to take the mind out of training. Shifting the individual's focus — perhaps by changing the rules, number of players, or size of the pitch — would change the stresses on the player. They embraced a decentralised approach to conditioning players as part of an overall system. The complexity is humbling, so we step away from shaping using our intellect or medical gadgets to try and shape or control complex systems.

José understood the concept of conditioning the whole athlete with the ball and on a football pitch. He had abandoned the long-running approach preferred by the Italian and French fitness coaches. He rejected the central mind approach, which trained players as if they were long-distance runners. This thinking is based on research papers focused on runners and their oxygen capacity.

Football is about skill under pressure. It is about being able to repeat that skill again and again in confined spaces under pressure while sprinting, jogging, or walking for an hour and a half. The central mind trains the body to be linear, on one plane of movement. It actually makes the player worse at football. We once worked with a fitness coach who was a former 200 m Olympic sprinter. When he got the ball during staff football matches, he couldn't change direction and would trip when he did. He was oriented vertically, just straight up and down.

He excelled in a one-dimensional sport — 200m. He was optimised to move in a straight line as fast as possible. His training was tuned to measuring one thing: time from A to B. Scientists love this as there are few variables, and it is almost like a sterile environment — no contaminants. However, football is chaos — constant change of directions with a bouncing ball, opponents, teammates, referee, rules, pitch, weather, etc., all needing control. Watching the sprinter try to adapt his linear conditioning to a chaotic environment was like watching Bambi on ice. Sports science is trying to isolate skills, making the athlete physically dumber.

Nature and the body cannot be isolated down into parts.

What I observed in José's system was to train the brain by placing massive pressure on each player's central nervous system and their ability to integrate into the complexity of the team. I witnessed firsthand how Chelsea FC transformed from an average professional team to an absolute beast of a team. José's training method honed the players' mental resilience, making them a formidable force on the football pitch.

Collectively, the team's central nervous systems were so conditioned that the players were almost calm under pressure. They were head and shoulders better than the other teams in the league. They went on to win everything, including the league title two seasons in a row. Again, it was very humbling. The doctors and fitness coaches love to get involved and show their importance. But in complex systems, you end up damaging the complexity of the billions of cells communicating via electrical signalling. Get the mind out of this!

The centralised mind so desperately wants to control everything, but it cannot comprehend the complexity of the body being decentralised. And that's even before we throw in perception and emotions, which we will explore later in the book.

The man who fixed Michael Jordan's knee

I got caught up in my self-importance when working with athletes. I used to tell players to keep their knees straight or keep their hips level, squeeze this or pull that. I was getting the athlete's mind involved, which is terrible for the body.

I learned to understand how the centralised mind gets involved and wrecks the decentralised system of the body. The moment the mind meddles with a complex system, it wreaks havoc.

For me, the concept of the all-powerful centralised mind was shattered that fateful day when I watched the player on the weight shift. When the player's emotion, his emotional thought, completely changed his body, a voice in my head screamed, "Oh my god, I know nothing about shit!"

When the student is ready, the teacher appears

I heard through Neil Day, a good friend of mine in football conditioning, about an unconventional physical therapist in America named Gary Gray. His story was fascinating. He had worked with Michael Jordan and helped him recover from his knee problem by finding the underlying cause of it. Spoiler alert: It was not the knee, by the way!

A fascinating sliver of this story grabbed my attention. Gary Gray lives in a small town in Michigan called Adrian. When Michael Jordan's agent had heard about this guy, supposedly the best therapist in the world, the agent called Gary and asked: "Can you fly in and help Michael Jordan with his knee?" Gary replied that he'd love to, but Michael would need to come to Adrian. He comes here, he stays with me, and we can get his knee better, Gary summarized. A true family man who wasn't changing for any superstar.

So Michael Jordan flew over in his private jet and stayed in Gary's home while he fixed his knee. That really struck me. Normally, people bow down to power and celebrity. Gary didn't. As a training professional, I was also struck by the way he allowed the wisdom of the body to refine itself through subtle adjustments to arms or legs, enhancing and improving deep movements. This process involved no mental intervention, which was exactly what I needed.

I heard Gary Grey created a Master's class in applied functional movement science. Compelled to learn more, I went to study with him in Adrian, Michigan. It was a wonderful experience and truly enlightening. One of the key lessons I took away from our time together was the importance of removing the mind from the body during movement. Instead of instructing someone to think about each movement consciously, Gary encouraged a different approach — movement is given and triggered by drivers. For instance, rather than saying, "Squat down and bend your knee," he would ask, "Can you reach down and touch that cone?" If the athlete touched the cone, then Gary would ask, "Can you reach up a little higher and over to the right?" or add "Look over there when you reach?" By providing specific tasks, the athlete's focus shifted away from conscious thinking, thus activating the body's innate drivers. What happens is because you have a task, there's no conscious, central mind trying to get involved in the unconscious movement of the body. This approach allowed the body to move naturally and unconsciously, generating more fluidity and efficient movements without interference from the central mind. In short, the body moves without thought.

In pure movement, the absence of a central authority is critical. When the mind intrudes, the body's responsiveness diminishes. This is evident in mixed martial arts. When fighters compete, they often attempt to manipulate each other emotionally — get in their opponent's head — to weaken their foe and gain an advantage. Conor McGregor is a perfect example. In one fight, McGregor riled José Aldo, his Brazilian opponent, so much so that Aldo over lunged out of anger and was knocked out in the first 6 seconds of the match. McGregor disrupted Aldo's flow state, pushing him into a mental, centrally controlled state.

The same concept applies to a sport like tennis. If your opponent is on fire and dominating with their forehand, generously praising their smoothness may inadvertently trigger the opposite thought: roughness. Their mind will analyse their forehand smoothness, causing them to manifest the opposite. Instantly, your words will jolt your opponent from flow to methodical analysis. Unless they are fortified against mental warfare and able to override your words, the once smooth forehand will dissolve into a frustrating attempt to regain dominance.

And so, working with Gary Gray taught me the importance of separating the centralised mind from the decentralised body. To excel, the body must act without conscious interference.

The ankle story — Negativity of the Centralised Mind

Writing this challenges me to discover more about myself. I have come to realise that when I discussed strategies with my colleagues in the medical team, we were, quite literally, speaking different languages. We operated in different paradigms.

I felt deep confusion when trying to explain concepts to them. I now understand the centralised mind cannot — and does not want to — give up its control and sense of importance. A cognitive dissonance.

"You can't measure a system within the same system."

— Jeff Booth

Unlike my peers, I approached work from a decentralised perspective and failed to recognise the opposing dynamic at play. I had been deeply conditioned with a behaviour of disappointment: not wanting to disappoint others or be a disappointment. And the more I fed that central conditioning by trying to escape it, the more deeply I experienced it. I felt disappointed in how I explained and stood up for myself, but also angry and disappointed at not being supported. Because I observed this feeling deeply and sought to understand its cause and effects, I no longer experience the internal storms around this behaviour of disappointment.

Fundamentally, science-based rehabilitation has an important place in athletic training. But when it comes to training an individual, you must adapt your approach to an individual's needs, both mentally and physically. Every person is unique.

Upon leaving Chelsea FC, I didn't have another job waiting for me, and my departure from the team was quite disappointing. (Precisely who was disappointed, I wasn't quite sure — again, that disappointment behaviour loop surfaced). I chose to resign when the team was not there, which meant I did not explain my decision to José and the players. I regret this. The next day, my then-girlfriend dumped me, which was very disappointing. She said I was a disappointment as a man. (Another disappointment behaviour loop) I will discuss behaviours later in the book and how to clear them.

While still out of a job, an ex-Chelsea footballer called me to ask if I would help him rehabilitate his ankle, which had broken down again after being treated by his club's medical team.

I remember feeling nervous going there to work with him, yet excited by the thought that my methods would be valued. To me, his call was a sign that the player lacked confidence in the medical team's evidence-based, central mind approach.

On our first day, I spoke to the fitness coach, who explained that the team's rehabilitation had been "amazing," but the athlete's his ankle was still not strong enough.

Curious about their approach, I asked what they were working on. The fitness coach explained that they were trying to improve the player's VO_2 max. To reach this abstract indicator of fitness, the team relied on a research paper that studied runners. The paper's conclusion suggested that training at four-minute intervals multiple times could boost an athlete's cardiovascular output.

Essentially, the medical team had the player running 1,000-meter repeats up to 10 times. The player is a massive, strong, and muscular defender. In a game, he has to, at the most, sprint for 10 meters, jump high and change direction quickly. But because the central authority of science had zero research on football defenders, the team determined that research on runners would be just as good. So, the fitness coach had the player do 1,000-meter repeats. He managed nine repeats until his ankle broke down.

Rather than training the athlete's ankle to perform multiple sprints maximally for 5 seconds each and change direction quickly, as in a football match, the ankle was forced to endure low-intensity impact for 4 minutes, nine times. And, predictably, because the player isn't a long-distance runner — he's much heavier and faster — his ankle broke down.

I was incredulous. Pacing in the changing room with this guy, I thought, "What the fuck! That is so fucking stupid. Am I missing something? That's the most fucking stupid thing I've ever heard." I didn't trust myself and questioned my own judgement against his previous medical professionals. (Remember my disappointment conditioning?) Looking back, I now realise they were sleepwalking through life, subjugating to the central dogma of science despite the potentially disastrous consequences of their actions.

Gaining confidence, I began the rehabilitation process, focusing on functional exercises designed to support the athletic demands and stresses of his position on the pitch. Once again, I encountered resistance from the medical team. They failed to grasp my approach, as it contradicted their rigid, central-minded dogma and established ways of learning. Unwilling to consider alternative methods, their ego seemed invested in their PhDs and group think. I had moved beyond their world and now saw the emperor wore no clothes. Bereft of mental sharpness, their dull minds swallowed confirmation-bias information without question.

Together, the player and I rehabilitated his ankle, and he returned to play in incredible shape. One day, as the medical team observed us at work, they caught him — just for a split second — have a slight problem with his ankle when moving backwards. This happens in rehab and is simply feedback for me to alter the exercise. The physiotherapists immediately stopped our work together. That was on Saturday. On Monday, he was doing full sprints. The manager, who happened to walk by when the player was mid-sprint, congratulated me on returning his athlete to peak performance. I could almost hear the physiotherapist grinding his teeth.

His recovery was an unmitigated success, and his ankle never broke down again. Yet, I came away from that experience extremely angry (and, of course, disappointed) because of how they treated me. With time, I began to understand the underlying psychology behind their behaviour. They were merely reflecting back to me my own deep disappointment and conditioned sense of helplessness.

In retrospect, it's obvious that their closed, centralised mind prevented them from being open and receptive to learning and understanding what their athlete's body truly needed. Our modern conditioning often leads us to yield to authority unquestioningly. In the case of the physiotherapy team, I found myself confused, putting their credentials above my own self-authority. I struggled to embrace my own expertise and self-authority.

Just as in the mental warfare of a tennis match, the moment we try to change ourselves or a complex system, like the body using the central mind, we will energise the opposite — what we are trying to move away from.

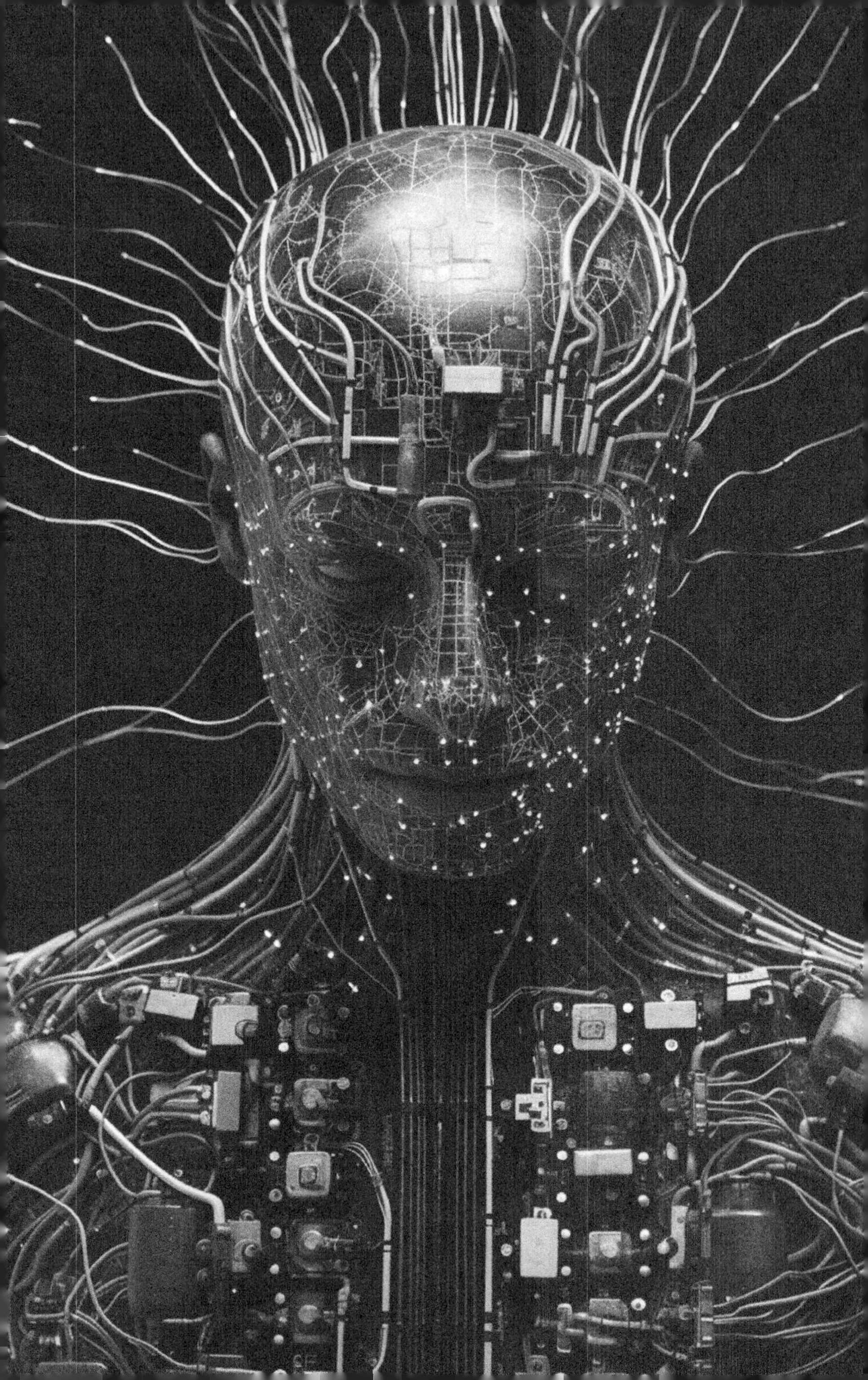

4

Mediation OS

Correcting the Centralised mind

My understanding of the centralised nature of the mind and its negative impact on the body was about to take a sharp detour down the rabbit hole.

By now, I was located in Spain, working with a footballer playing for FC Barcelona. My primary quest became to replicate the energy shift phenomenon I previously discovered while working with the Chelsea Football Club player. I was looking for a way to tap into the strong and weak energy that control an athlete's body. This search led me to study several different energy-based modalities, from Tai Chi, Qigong, Body Talk, touch therapies, massage, tapping, hypnosis, etc. But none of these modalities offered both the reparative accuracy and speed that I had experienced. Fundamentally, they all were based on the paradigm that healing takes a certain amount of time.

Interestingly, I had been plagued with back pain since I left Chelsea. The pain was constant, especially intense when waking in the morning. It had progressed to the point where even simple tasks, like going to the toilet, became excruciating. I vividly recall crawling to the toilet and putting my hand on my knee to lift the toilet seat to manage the severe pain. It was while I was studying these modalities to resolve my own pain, my own anxieties, and my own insecurities that I recognized that I could use this research to guide others. I had been to Olympic massage therapists, chiropractors, and physios worldwide from Paris to LA. No one could pinpoint the underlying cause. I even paid a renowned holistic health practitioner $10,000 to fix my back or at least work out why I had that problem. But he couldn't resolve it either.

Then, on one fortuitous day, I came across Dr. Kam Yuen from America, though I can't recall exactly how I first heard about him. It's possible that in my endless search for answers, I had watched a video about or by him years ago. Still, here he was, in my YouTube feed, audaciously claiming he could resolve anything on the spot instantly. Something inside nudged me . . . let me give this guy a try.

Dr. Yuen's assertions that he could solve my problems without even speaking to me seemed farcical. Rather, all I was required to do was describe my issues briefly by typing a few sentences into a box. Sceptical as I was, I complied and wrote about my morning back pain and recurring calf muscle tears when running.

With a payment of $40 and a brief description of my problem typed in the designated box, Dr. Yuen claimed he could resolve my ailments. Quite frankly, I didn't believe his promises and wasn't particularly hopeful about the outcome. Nevertheless, I thought, "Why not give it a shot for 40 bucks?" A short time after pressing "send," I received a reply: Your weaknesses come from your sternum, you have some karma of breaking people's backs, and you have spiritual experiences of being hit by sharp objects when you are running away, like spears.

The morning after the teleclinic, I awakened with zero back pain. It was gone! I could not feel any pain. As I listened to the recording he made, he repeated what I had written and said I am weak to the bed, to the horizontal position.

I was stunned. I could hardly believe it. I waited for the back pain to return, but it never did. Dr. Yuen had resolved it. Awed, I remained silent in my mind, with my eyes darting around, scrambling for answers the entire day. When it finally sank in that my back pain was genuinely gone and not returning, an epiphany spread throughout my mind and body. I knew that whatever Dr. Yuen was doing, his approach based on strong and weak principles, the binary concept of one and zero, was the very thing I had been relentlessly seeking for many, many years.

A new path had arrived. I immersed myself in his body of work. I read all his books. I listened to every interview and every podcast, and there are many of them. For the next three years, I digested everything Dr. Kam Yuen had touched- all day, every day. I was obsessed.

To fully absorb his work, I did what I know that I'm good at: breaking down the fundamental principles and then applying them myself. I listened to what he was doing, and then I started to do it on myself, repeatedly and obsessively. I walked for hours listening to him and then turning off the audio and doing this energy system on myself constantly.

Without hesitation, I began implementing this newfound approach on others, experimenting and putting it to the test. As I delved deeper, I incorporated this method into my client's physical therapy treatment protocols. What astonished me was the realisation that this one and zero coding was precisely what the football player had demonstrated on the scales earlier. Positive, reinforcing thoughts seemed to fortify his central nervous system, the core of his electrical body, while negative thoughts produced a palpable weakening effect, creating a weak current throughout his body. It became evident that this non-physical process had a profound impact on the body's energy dynamics, aligning perfectly with what I had observed during the football player's session on the scales.

As I integrated this philosophy into my life and work, I developed a keen awareness of a strong and weak sensation in my body. To better explain this concept, I can borrow the phrase "internal physiological sensitivity" as described in Josh Waitzkin's excellent book, *The Art of Learning*, which details his experience as a champion in the eastern art of pushing hands. Drawing from my experiences with Tai Chi and Qigong, I found it relatively easy to grasp this notion. Through these practices, I learned to discern the strength and weakness of various positions of my feet, hands, wrists, and fingers in relation to my energy. For instance, in Tai Chi and Qigong, I discovered that turning my hands toward my body produced a strengthening effect, while turning them away weakened my energy. Similarly, pointing my feet inwards strengthened me, whereas pointing them outwards weakened me. This heightened sensitivity to my body's internal responses allowed me to calibrate and refine my understanding of the strong and weak dynamics at play within the body.

At first, the most difficult thing was to feel the difference between strength and weakness while asking myself questions. This was because my centralised mind kept popping in and derailing my awareness. "Are you sure that's weak?" "This can't be true. It's a con, and woo-woo!"

I kept at it, though, ignoring my mind's invasive questions and instead listening to the results. For example, improving the range of a tight ankle or removing pain in a shoulder joint would tell me if strengthening from a weak to strong energy was effective. I avoided relying on conditional beliefs that perceive us as separate entities like robots, a mindset influenced by Newtonian science. Instead, I embraced a more interconnected perspective, acknowledging the subtle energies that can influence our well-being and functionality. My focus on real, observable results allowed me to progress and validate the efficacy of the composite approach.

You can experience this phenomenon yourself. Go inward, into your internal space, and focus on your torso. Think of something you are deeply proud of... As you do, pay attention to the physical sensations you experience inside your torso. Now, shift your thoughts to the worst day of your life and notice how your torso responds. Compare the two. There is a difference, right?

For me, when I think of the proud thought, I feel my energy rise near the top of my torso, and I sense a tightening. When I think of the second thought, that feeling drops low in my torso, almost like an energy plug has been pulled. The calmer and quieter you are, the easier these sensations are to detect.

The analogy I like to use is a calm sea, so calm it's like oil. One could sense a single drop of water if it fell into its mirror surface. Now imagine a rough sea and try to sense a single drop. You probably couldn't feel a *barrel* drop into it.

That's the problem with humans today: we are distracted. Our minds are so stimulated by social media, junk food, and stimulants that it's almost impossible to perceive anything so subtle.

Mastering this internal technology requires developing sensitivity to perceive the subtle differences between strong and weak energies, represented by the binary concept of 1 and 0. The key is to train our ability to quickly assess these sensations, allowing no space for feeling our emotions, as they would disrupt the technique's efficacy. To achieve the ability to resolve emotions instantly, we must be attuned to both the strong and weak energy states.

To this day, I remain unclear how this technique accomplishes what it does. While I have some theories, my primary focus lies in achieving tangible results with my clients, not discovering the exact mechanics of its functionality. Ultimately, science will catch up and shed light on the underlying process, whether it involves photons in cells or the interaction of electrical signals in the mitochondrial electron transport system reacting to our consciousness.

"Any sufficiently advanced technology is indistinguishable from magic".

— Arthur C. Clarke

As I dug into Dr. Yuen's methodology from a Western science perspective, I encountered difficulties in finding corroborative evidence for traditional Chinese medicine principles. Western medicine tends to adopt a mechanistic view, perceiving the body's anatomy as separate objects with little interconnectedness.

Through exploration, I discovered that the body's unconscious coordination was profoundly more decentralised than I had ever imagined. I began to discern that the underlying causes and sources of physical problems were rooted in non-physical factors. And that this interconnectedness reaches far beyond one's body, weaving itself into the universe.

What struck me the most about the brief session with Kam was how it felt as though he had gained remote access to my 'computer,' which he could access and maintain from a distance. This notion shattered the idea of separation among human beings. We exist on a humankind blockchain, interconnected, with no true division among us.

Still today, I remain captivated by the concept of strong and weak energy, the foundational one and zero coding underpinning everything. It fascinated me how the slightest misalignment in this code generated an immediate effect on the physical body, reinforcing the dynamic interplay in the energies of well-being. Much like a website viewed on a computer, there is no point shouting at the screen to shift a wrongly positioned photo; you must dig in and alter the corresponding source code to actuate lasting change.

Interfacing with the Meditation OS

During my journey, I learned that pain does not exist in a body part but is located in our brains. Our perception governs how painful something is, and perception is a control mechanism embedded in the brain.

Consider a baker whose left hand was mangled and later amputated whilst making bread. Months later the doctors continued to be puzzled as the baker complained of extreme pain in his phantom hand, but only on Saturdays. Everyone was at a loss. One day, the baker realised that it was on Saturdays when fresh bread was baked, and the smell of the fresh bread wafting through the bakery triggered the traumatic event.

In pain science, this event is identified as a neural tag triggered by an "Ignition Cue." Suspecting there was more behind the science, I dug deeper into the rabbit hole, guided by one of the most difficult clients I have ever worked with.

The Skeptic Who Found His Swing

An ex-professional footballer paid for the session, and what I didn't realise was that the client was a staunch atheist and that anything that whiffed of religion or woo-woo would be unceremoniously dismissed. He didn't suffer fools lightly.

We connected via Skype, and he greeted me in shorts ready for the series of exercises he expected me to oversee. I thought, "Oh shit!" I kindly explained that I wasn't going to prescribe specific exercises or stretches, but rather, I intended to talk with him and assess his energy to find out where he was weak. His face dropped. Although he kept assuring me that he felt no differences and that the pain was excruciating, we spent the next hour identifying sources of energy, strength and weakness.

At the conclusion, he stated, and I quote, "You are a very nice person, but that was the biggest waste of an hour in my entire life." I walked away from that session bruised and chalked it up to experience.

Two weeks later, I received a message from the footballer asking how the session had gone with his friend. I laughed and explained what had happened. He was surprised by the story, as he had just seen his friend playing golf, something the friend had been unable to do for many years because of his back pain.

I was confused but nonplussed.

Two months later, the client reached out... The first thing he told me was, "You're weird. You're spooky!" Surprised and amazed, he proceeded to tell me that he hadn't been in touch since our session because the session had upended him; it had shaken his core beliefs. He shared that the day after the session, he awakened with no back pain for the first time in 19 years. Prior to this, he had undergone multiple surgeries and relied on heavy pain meds due to this documented medical condition. But now, the pain was simply gone.

He couldn't believe it, so he mowed the lawn, which used to always hurt. Nothing. So he then decided to drive to the Isle of Man; that would hurt his back for sure. Nothing. He was flabbergasted. He could not understand how I could have done that with no touch while being in another country.

The process really was remarkable. The things that I found as 'tags' were not as simple as smells like the baker's or even a visual trigger. They were deep traumas from his ancestors that were being stored as deep memories and encoded down through generations. Once I switched them from weakening to strengthening his body, the pain disappeared. Like all pain, it had little to do with his back but simply a way for his body to show him that he harboured some tremendously painful weaknesses deep within his code.

What struck me as particularly intriguing and reassuring about this session was that this client was a complete non-believer. He held no bias or preconceived notion that I possessed magic powers or some mythical cure. In fact, he had dismissed the session entirely. Extremely opinionated, nothing had ever swayed this client's belief system until he woke up and his 19 years of pain had vanished.

The GPS of Your Mind

The crucial aspect of this remarkable outcome was that it worked without any placebo effect. This was of utmost importance to me because I didn't want to work in a system that required a belief to trigger the change. My aim was to understand and apply first principles, seeking genuine truth in affecting instantaneous transformations. Witnessing such a profound shift in someone who had been sceptical from the outset reinforced the authenticity and potency of the approach I was exploring. It seemed to work without a placebo effect, and that was vital because I wasn't interested in messing around with something that needed a belief in it to work. I wanted the first principles of truth that I was affecting change on something that made a change instantly.

Through this experience, I grasped the necessity of engaging with the decentralised energy system using a 1 and 0 energy framework that served as a GPS to hone in on the primary weakness. Predictably, when my centralised mind, beliefs, and conditioning intruded and dictated solutions, the approach's effectiveness diminished. To succeed, I had to maintain absolute neutrality to the session's outcome, made possible by tapping into my decentralised mind.

The pinnacle of this method's unbiased nature manifested in one of the most significant accomplishments of my career. This achievement underscored the power and authenticity of the approach when liberated from personal biases or preconceived notions.

As I embraced decentralised thinking, patterns in tags and descriptions emerged, reminding me of the spiritual books I had read when I first ventured into this realm. These books explored the concept that the physical pain experienced in different parts of the body served as signposts, pointing to struggles within our unconscious minds. Once identified, the signposts could be mapped and explored.

With my understanding of body energy growing, I began looking closely at how my clients described their physical ailments and mapped them to how they experienced stress in other areas. This technique had been part of my process since my time at Chelsea FC, but, at that time, I lacked the insight to collect and assimilate this information effectively. But I did now.

Interestingly, at about the same time, pain research by the modern Western medical establishment began inching closer to what I was observing. Still light years behind, but a sliver of enlightenment was peeking through.

Lorimer Mosely, a world-renowned expert in pain science, delivers great lectures on the complexity of pain. In one such lecture, accessible on YouTube, he shared a story about a man who was bitten by a snake while walking in a forest. At first, the man thought it was a twig, and the pain was mild. But the moment he saw the snake, the pain became excruciating. His perception of the incident triggered the pain signal in his brain. Weeks later, the same man was again walking in the forest, and his leg grazed against a twig. He experienced immediate and extreme pain as his brain reconnected to the snake tag created just weeks earlier. Remarkably, when his brain processed that it was just a twig, the pain quickly subsided.

I may have butchered the story somewhat, so don't come after me on Twitter, but the underlying message is accurate. Pain is perceived and processed in the brain, and the intensity and duration are based on how threatening the event is to you.

Instinctively, I have believed in this hardwired brain-pain connection for decades. Through greater understanding, though, I have come to realise that if a person is struggling to move forward in their life, whether it's with changing careers or starting a business, the pain will surface in their knees or lower limbs. Think of it this way: They want to put the right foot forward but are worried about doing the wrong thing. Fear. The brain cannot distinguish between the mental fear of taking a step and when the person is physically stepping forward. This may seem crazy, but it's what I have seen and resolved by directing the client to the truth behind the manifested symptom.

Here's another groundbreaking discovery. The moment you uncover the truth, the actual underlying case behind a pain in the body, it instantly resolves. Yes, instantly. Now, I'm not talking about a bone sticking out of the leg type of pain. At that moment, you require emergency care and likely surgery. I'm talking about back pain, numbness, and other bodily discomforts.

Imagine you are a consultant tasked with diagnosing a malfunctioning computer. You would not suggest that the owner leave it untouched for weeks and expect it to miraculously heal itself: "Leave the computer with me for 4 weeks, so it heals." That would be crazy. Instead, you would diligently search for the glitch in the operating system or in the software and resolve it. The moment you find the truth behind the problem, the glitch will be resolved. The same applies to business; identifying the truth behind a lack of productivity allows for resolution.

While medicine has made remarkable advancements in areas like surgeries, heart care, and bone repair, it lags behind when it comes to mental health and pain resolution. This disparity is far more significant than we may realise. I believe that sometime in the next century, we'll look back at this era as a dark age in medicine, especially in mental health and pain management. Within these realms lie great potential for unlocking the interconnectedness of the mind and body, and embracing these opportunities will pave the way for more holistic approaches to health and wellness.

In another example of mind-body connectedness, I once had a client from Australia who had been grappling with post-traumatic stress disorder (PTSD) for an agonising three years. Despite seeking help from a therapist, she still struggled daily with the distressing effects of PTSD.

She agreed to approach the situation from a new perspective. We engaged in a one-hour-long session. During this session, I identified the factors that weakened her and worked on weeding them out. Remarkably, we reduced her fears to zero. One month later, we met for a follow-up session. When I inquired about her PTSD symptoms, she smiled and shared that they had completely vanished since our initial session. Now, she wanted to discuss a relationship issue. Over a year passed, and we spoke again, and her PTSD had never returned.

The client's astonishing story spurred me to share it on a forum, hoping to inspire others. Sadly, a psychologist reprimanded me, claiming it was dangerous to suggest that PTSD could be resolved in one session and that the client was probably lying. The psychologist's reaction, however, was predictable. One cannot easily comprehend a new system if you are entrenched in an old one. This is especially true when the new paradigm challenges strongly held beliefs and revered authority, particularly if you are the authority and you derive income from your status. My client's experience completely disrupted the psychologist's model, so she defaulted to her own form of denial. This is the way of systems.

> *"The system will always be defended by those countless people with enough intellect to defend, but not quite enough to innovate."*
>
> — Edward de Bono

Energy, Past and Present

This brings me to one client, for I still am in awe of how this strong and weak energy can work. I was contacted by a lady in the UK whose daughter had been diagnosed with liver cirrhosis; she was born with this incurable disease. The mother explained that her daughter was on a waiting list for a transplant, and she would probably die within a year if this didn't happen. At the age of one, a liver transplant was a very difficult operation to do.

I remember clearly this first session where she held up her beautiful little daughter, who had a huge distended belly. I couldn't see the whites of her eyes because of jaundice. She was a very sick child. She held her up, and said, "Please, Rob, please help save my daughter."

Her daughter was the same age as my daughter at the time, and tears came to my eyes. It was a very emotional moment. I remember thinking, how on earth can what I do affect such a sick, medically diagnosed incurable disease? I explained to her that I didn't know if I could help her child, but I could try looking for all the weaknesses affecting the baby. She pleaded, "Please, please, please."

So, over the next few weeks and months, we did a session nearly every week. All we had to go on were the hospital records of her blood tests, her white blood cell count, etc. Quite quickly, the numbers started to improve, and the doctors weren't sure what was happening. Every session, I focused on finding out where the weak energy was coming from. Was it coming from the baby? Or was it coming from the mother or father or from somewhere else?

All I was doing was finding and weeding out weaknesses. Within a few months, the doctors started to ask the mother what she was doing because her daughter was starting to get much better. The numbers were coming back to normal. The doctor said, "We don't know what's happening. But don't get your hopes up. There's no cure for this."

Around one year after we started working together, I was on holiday in Majorca at the time. The mother called me telling me she had been for a checkup, and the doctor said we didn't know what had happened, but all the scans showed that there was no more sclerosis of the liver. The liver is perfect. They used the word 'miraculous'. They've never seen anything like that. They couldn't explain what had happened.

By this time, the mother no longer listened to them. Her daughter was cured. This was very emotional work for me. I became close to the family. It was fulfilling on a professional level, too. It made me realise how powerful this one and zero underpinning energy is to the health of humans.

In all the sessions, I worked through the mother and her perception of her child. The baby was sometimes in the sessions, but fundamentally, the baby didn't know what I was talking about. She couldn't speak. She was either asleep or playing around or not there.

I realised that I didn't need the baby or the client to believe in what I was doing, although the mother did, and the baby was completely cured of her sclerosis anyway. Now that child is six, it's a very heart-warming and remarkable experience that I will never forget.

Rebooting to Meditation OS

Writing this book has allowed me to reflect on the skills I have honed over the past 15 years. My life's passion revolves around treating people like a computer system. The body is the hardware, the mind is the software, and the internet connection represents the area outside the mind, encompassing empathic abilities to connect with others' emotions or ancestral traumas via a coded energy network.

My work is such that I can work with anyone in the world,

anywhere, anytime. I have revived a professional MMA fighter's numb left arm in a hotel room in Shanghai in 10 minutes by finding the underlying cause: suppressed emotions around his father. The fighter had previously been advised that the numbness emanated from his neck and that he would need to retire. During our hotel room session, the Brazilian fighter pleaded, "Please, Robbi, I love to fight. Please help me." With the numbness completely resolved, and in his fight, he knocked his opponent down with a sharp *left* hook from the arm we had worked on.

Even a WhatsApp call from a changing room can yield success. A professional footballer in Asia pulled his hamstring during warm-up and was going to miss the match. During our WhatsApp session in the changing room, I found that the player had connected with the emotions of his manager, who was close to losing his job. I worked on this weakness, and the pain in the hamstring disappeared. He played that day and earned man of the match. I cherish the screenshot of the WhatsApp conversation to this day.

Even as I marvel at the incredible results, I remain driven to seek further improvements. This pursuit also posed a challenge, as my insatiable desire for progress leaves me feeling unsatisfied at times. A nagging query continued to ricochet in my brain: Why can't I lessen or remove the pain for everyone?

I had identified that those who were resistant to permanent improvement were people who were dealing with addiction or deep personality behaviours that proved challenging to modify. The question of why their strong energy couldn't be maintained persisted until a pivotal moment about a year and a half ago. It dawned on me that the key lay in addressing not just the "computer" (the body and mind) but also the "person" operating it — the centralizing, conditioned mind that exerted control.

Contemplating this revelation led me to discover what I termed the "decentralised mind." The decentralised mind was the missing piece to unlock deeper transformations in individuals dealing with complex issues. With this realisation, I embarked on a new phase of my journey, ready to explore the potential and power of the decentralised mind in facilitating profound changes and personal growth.

5

Centralised to Decentralised Mind

Recently, I had the privilege of working with a world-renowned client, someone who seemed to have it all — wealth, success, and a towering reputation. During our session, it became apparent that beneath the façade of achievement, he was deeply unhappy and burnt out. Despite attaining immense wealth and leaving a lasting impact on the world, he felt trapped and devoid of joy in his career and life.

He had certainly achieved his goals, founding a large financial company and owning a sports club and had acquired more money than he could ever spend. In our session, we explored his drives and motivations, uncovering a powerful realisation. He understood that his pursuit of money was, in fact, a quest for something deeper — freedom. Money had become synonymous with freedom in his mind, shedding light on the root of his discontent.

Freedom was important to him because he detested limitations of any kind and loathed being told what to do. He was never really interested in the wealth itself but in what he perceived as the power it gave him, giving him freedom from limitations. So, his deep drive for money was really a drive to avoid limitations at any cost. But from where had this seed germinated? Memories of a bitter, old, discontented father, constantly complaining and seething from his armchair, had left a profound impact on him. He spent his life driven to become the antithesis of his father. His voice cracked, and his body slumped when he realised that he had, in fact, become like his father.

Put simply, he was jammed up. His energy was blocked around freedom and enslavement. Enslavement and limitation was the binary 1 and 0 energy flow that weakened him. Throughout his life, critical decisions had driven him to move towards freedom, yet he energised the opposite — limitation and enslavement — two paths that stored his weakness.

In the realm of shaping one's life through internal emotional drives, it's crucial to recognize the influence of the mind's duality, represented by the yin and yang principles. In this way, you energise the opposite of what you seek. It's akin to a metaphorical hamster wheel — a cycle where one expends tremendous effort to move in one direction only to find oneself inevitably drawn back into the other direction. Here, the drive toward freedom pulled my client back to enslavement. Often, individuals try to escape certain aspects of their lives that they disapprove of or have grown tired of but face the same issues repeatedly. This pattern persists because the centralised mind tends to reinforce the very things one wishes to change, acting as a sort of glitch in the metaphorical matrix.

True enlightenment lies in understanding this phenomenon

and transitioning to a decentralised mindset. By doing so, a person can break free from the constraints of the familiar and live a more harmonious life, unshackled by the contradictory forces within their own mind. This newfound shift in perspective allows individuals to liberate themselves from repetitive patterns and embrace a state of peace and freedom.

This principle is also rooted in Buddhism. Buddha aptly describes this mind trap as the squirrel cage, symbolising how we become ensnared in the illusion of samsara, the centralised mind. In this analogy, the squirrel ceaselessly tries to improve itself, aspiring toward the zenith, unaware that it is energising the opposite, the nadir. Buddha saw this truth thousands of years ago, and dedicated his life to observing his own behaviours and thoughts until he achieved enlightenment. In doing so, he gained a deep understanding of the centralised mind's illusory nature and rejected it in favour of a decentralised state. This transformative shift can be metaphorically described as undressing the layers of illusion, culminating in enlightenment.

Before he passed, Buddaha strived to help others see the value of his path by explaining that you cannot find enlightenment by following others; you must become your own self-authority. Do not worship me. However, the conditioning is deep in us humans, and soon, followers erected a huge golden Buddha to worship.

On a personal note, I learned of the concept of the squirrel cage, zenith, and nadir just this year. Discovering these profound concepts brought a deep sense of reassurance, as I had independently arrived at similar conclusions through my personal endeavours and proof of work observations. These first principles of our internal landscapes aligned with the insights of Buddha and other sages comforted me, an ordinary man attempting to understand and free myself from humanity's programming. The more I undo and unlearn centralisation, the more I enjoy myself and those around me. This pursuit is the greatest, most meaningful work I can do to reduce the violence and ugliness in the world. Through decentralisation, I am able to love myself, others, and my whole environment more, bringing profound cleansing and harmony to all of humanity.

The Bitcoin Mind

Our deeply conditioned behaviours and motivations lie at the base layer of all humans. Everything above it, our reality out there, is regulated by this level, like a decentralised blockchain with all human conditioning inside of it. We are like nodes, with all of the human conditioning written within this blockchain.

In explaining these concepts to the client, I emphasised that he is his own self-authority; he holds his own keys. He must keenly observe the patterns in his deep unconscious blockchain to gain personal insight. By recognizing these patterns, the tyranny they hold over him will dissolve. This is because the observer is the observed. There is no separation. I cautioned against reacting negatively to his observations or labelling them as wrong because this reinforces the centralised mind. Trying to avoid or replace these behaviours creates conflict and perpetuates the cycle, leading to emotional imprisonment.

Conversely, embracing the whole and self-awareness will pave the way to liberation and inner peace. A genuine understanding of this truth goes beyond mere intellectual comprehension. When we deeply grasp that what we observe is a reflection of ourselves, with no separation, we move into a profound experience of life — We embrace the entirety of reality and embody the truth. When the central mind structure (the ego) is seen and understood, it dissolves, leaving behind the liberated decentralised mind.

Remember that a problem perceived within the centralised mind cannot be altered by the very system that gave rise to it. Any attempt to change it, whether by pursuing a positive direction, avoiding a negative one, or even choosing to say, "Screw it, I'll do nothing," is a movement that reinforces that behaviour.

Humanity's collective movement from a centralised to a decentralised mind will be the greatest revolution humankind can experience. Why do I say this?

We, in the modern world, have not changed psychologically in millennia. Our technology has, but our minds still operate in the centralised game. Even with all the religions, gurus, and authorities trying to shape us, the societal structure that governs us has remained unchanged. The already semi-enlightened offer a path to truth. If you follow this book or that doctrine, you will find truth and freedom. However, this is absurd; there is no path to truth. Just like bitcoin exploded outwards and decentralised, so must our learning explode out in every moment so we can decentralise and understand ourselves.

In following others, we no longer learn for ourselves. We become dull and inflexible.

This is why I'm so fascinated by bitcoin. I believe it is a psychological trojan horse that will shift human consciousness. To me, it serves as the orange pill, leading us on a transformative journey towards the red pill — a deeper understanding of reality. Many fellow bitcoin enthusiasts have shared how their initial attraction was financial gain, only to tumble down the rabbit hole of discovering how the true nature of money and corrupt societal structure suppress humanity. The Wizard of Oz cunningly tricked his people into believing him all-powerful until Toto arrived and swept the curtain aside, revealing the decaying core of our financial and societal systems. Toto is bitcoin.

Bitcoin awakens the human consciousness, sparking a newfound awareness around our conditioning related to money, work, and government. As a result, we find ourselves questioning every aspect of our lives. This ripple effect extends into every aspect of a bitcoiner's life. Through the lens of bitcoin, we re-examine the centralised governance structures that shape our societies, from the top-down educational system and the flawed medical establishment to the practices of organised religious institutions. The profound impact of bitcoin's awakening reverberates throughout our entire perception of the world.

This is the orange pill. Powerful.

My perception of reality seems to be changing at an ever-increasing pace. This red pill strips away the conditioned structure in my mind, and I take great responsibility for finding the truth about my conditioning.

My experience informs me that all physical reality is underpinned by consciousness, also known as the base layer. This layer gets fractured when we attach ourselves to beliefs, social norms, and rules, distorting our perspective on life. If we want to alter our experiences, we must address the root cause. In other words, if we want to watch a different film, we can't just change the screen. We must change the film reel and the input. I must clarify that I am not referring to marketing tactics like the 'law of attraction,' which entice centralised minds with the false promise of control in the game of life. While there is some truth to the concept that we attract what we energise, we are inevitably drawn to the opposite of what we desire.

I posit that the most significant centralization and tyranny we face today lies much closer to home. It lurks within our centralised minds, as the dystopian movie *The Matrix* depicted. In our lives, we, too, are caught in a matrix, a virtual reality of our own making. It is similar to a computer program populated by our human conditioning, and it controls us.

Incredibly, our fundamental psychology hasn't changed in thousands of years. True, technology has shifted, but as humans, we haven't changed one bit. If we want to change this wretched world, we must see the centralised prison within ourselves and migrate towards a decentralised mind. We must understand that we are humans on our very own decentralised blockchain and that 'out there' is no different than 'in here'.

All human conditioning is written and encoded on this decentralised human blockchain. For us to change the contents of the blockchain, each one of us must take responsibility for all of human conditioning. To change ourselves is to change society. A shift of this magnitude will be our greatest revolution. Everyone and I have our role to play because the observer is the observer.

If we see violence, hatred, greed, and suffering out there, we must look for that in ourselves. If we try to change and shape out there using the centralised mind, we will manifest the opposite. If we want to create good, we will create evil. We are wholly responsible for the entirety of the human condition.

Throughout history, whenever experts have attempted to mould and control human behaviour, imposing the principles of centralised minds on decentralised systems, their efforts have consistently met with failure.

Examples abound, such as scientists introducing vegetarian piranhas to aid the locals in Papua New Guinea, only to end up with carnivorous piranhas destroying the lake's ecosystem. Now, the once thriving community is impoverished, unable to swim or fish in the lake anymore. Similarly, the Catholic Church, once seen as a force for good, has faced grievous deviations, concealing heinous acts of paedophilia, facilitating Nazi passports, and covering up the genocide in Rwanda — among other grave transgressions. These instances are stark reminders of how well-intentioned, centralised efforts veer tragically off course when not in harmony with the decentralised nature of humanity.

To my client, who desired freedom above all but had become imprisoned by the very rewards of his endeavours, know that the central mind seduces us and tricks us into the never-ending hamster wheel. Be comforted that when you shine light into this darkness, you realise the danger, and if you see a snake enter your house, you do not take your eyes off it. When we deeply understand that the observer is the observed, then there is no separation between what's inside of us and what's out there. Only then will we experience the most beautiful freedom.

Thus, the moment you want to change something about yourself, or you want to achieve something, or move away from something, simply watch the behaviour. This counterintuitive non-movement is so powerful yet so difficult for humans because of the very conditioning they are responding to.

I recently had a fascinating discovery session with the founder and CEO of a company in the bitcoin space. We changed pleasantries, and then I switched into treasure-hunter mode, digging for hints of gold that would lead me to his innermost vault. Extremely intelligent, he could spar with any philosopher in the world on complex technical and philosophical concepts. However, he felt burnt out, lacked motivation, and suffered from procrastination. I explained that these were simply symptoms of a hidden manacle — smoke to a fire whose fuel must be found.

I drilled down into his procrastination and listened closely for repeated words. Then I heard, "I am unable to move forward," and "I am stuck." The hamster wheel of *Able* and *Unable*. He was desperately peddling the wheel to be able. As he did that, he kept flipping to the opposite — unable.

I explained the nature of the centralised mind and its duality, and we started a little game of looking for this behaviour in different areas of his life. It was literally in all areas, from his thoughts around his business, his wife and kids, and his health. Even his corporate mission aimed toward helping customers become more able while moving away from being unable.

He acknowledged he was plagued by thoughts of "I am not doing enough of ______." and "I should be doing more ______." Fill in the blanks (maybe you can relate to this behaviour). We humans are conditioned the same way, just to varying degrees.

Because of the inner torment, he had become utterly exhausted by this recurring behaviour, 'incapable' (unable) of changing it. Within his centralised mind, he saw two options. The first was to become more able, enhance his abilities. The second involved seeking distraction and escape through pleasures or substances, creating a temporary distance from the issue. Giving up could also be an option, but then he would experience complete unable-ness (inability). At that moment, he realised he had been trapped on this wheel his entire life, completely unaware of his mind's hidden prison bars.

I reminded him that he was his own self-authority and that his behaviour was like having a dangerous snake in his house. He must now keep his eyes on the behaviour and watch it laser-focused to understand it and only it. He must not try to change or move away from it. Understand it, and it will dissolve. The hardest thing to do, yet the simplest.

He then asked me, "What would be the best way to do this? ...." Knowing he would ask, I interrupted him and said: "Look at what you just asked me." He chuckled and quickly realised this was the "unable" behaviour taking over again.

Remember, this behaviour does not want to be seen, and it

demands to be fed to reinforce itself and grow. Shining light into this darkness will set you free.

This pattern of unable-able behaviour can be observed in many high performers. It drives them to greatness in their boldness, but inevitably, they will experience profound uselessness.

Another way to frame the concept of watching the centralised mind is to imagine having an internal dojo. I often explain to students in my course that a dojo resides in our heads. Also inside this mental space is an opponent, a hybrid beast, and Ronin standing opposite. The hideous beast will attack us with endless emotional problems throughout our lives, its katana hacking repeatedly. But the sword will be rendered impotent, swinging through us without harm, if we simply observe the experience without reacting — no movement to fight or change the situation. Any pain we experience is because we have a wound or weakness within us, a faulty code that tags the sword.

To eliminate this weakness, we can strengthen it through lightning meditation and then return to the practice of observing. Our greatest peace and success will come when we activate our Meditation OS via non-doing, no commenting, simply observing the behaviour. By doing so, we starve the behaviour of the food it requires to maintain its control over us. Without sustenance, it then dissolves away. Wu Wei, effortless non-doing.

Through my own experiences, I have understood that the greatest power lives within us. And this power holds the potential for the ultimate revolution for mankind.

"If you want to awaken all of humanity, then awaken

all of yourself. If you want to eliminate the suffering in the world, then eliminate all that is dark and negative in yourself. Truly, the greatest gift you have to give is that of your own self-transformation."

— Lao Tzu

6

UnParenting

If I was to pinpoint the area of my life that has been the most profoundly affected by observing my behaviour, it would unequivocally be as a parent to my children.

I did not intend to address parenting in this book, but as I gathered my thoughts, I realised the act of parenting is where I spend most of my time observing my behaviour.

Just yesterday, my daughter, Lima, was jumping on the bed. We have been trying to teach her a bedtime routine of brushing her teeth and getting her pyjamas on. Like any parent at this stage, this wasn't my first rodeo, and I knew the emotional storm inside was about to be triggered.

I asked her if she could stop jumping and get ready for bed, and as you probably can guess, she ignored me and continued playing. Now, did you see how I described what happened? I perceived that she had ignored me, triggering an inability to get through to her and me being able to have things the way I wanted. This girl, with only six years on this planet, was fully involved in jumping and was not listening to anything.

Rather than viewing her behaviour as typical for a six-year-old, I perceived I was being ignored. I felt a deep helplessness within me and reacted to it by getting frustrated. I wanted to push her to behave the way I wanted. I repeated the request several times until I started to get angry. I observed this anger and inability to see clearly, and I observed a need to punish her for "not doing as she was told" by her father.

It is difficult, when the behaviour starts to take over, to stay in a decentralised position and observe the behaviour of the centralised mind. But because I have been doing this for a while, I was able to walk away and into another room to watch my behaviour without being triggered further. My self-administered timeout only took one minute. Then, when I could clearly see this behaviour was controlling me, it started to dissolve.

I walked back into the room and explained that I wanted to go to bed because I was tired, but I understood that she loved jumping on the bed, so what solution could we devise, a compromise? She heard that, and I told her that I would like to read Harry Potter and that I'd like to read it together. She agreed, and the evening routine went on its way.

I knew that resorting to punishment and asserting my authority as her father could have left my daughter feeling subjugated, which would have created a deep sense of helplessness within her. This feeling of helplessness would eventually erode the trust she has in me and caused her to reject the illusion of my authority. Instead of nurturing her innate capabilities, I would have imposed a coercive force, depriving her of her innate *able*-ness.

Coercion is deeply ingrained within all of us. I see it in both my family's and my wife's family behaviours. Coercion can be subtle like taking away attention from the child when they don't do as the adult wants, to passive-aggressive threats like refusing to buy something, or even physically moving the child to where the adult wants to go. Fundamentally, these tactics manipulate the child to get the outcome the adult wants.

The pattern of authority-driven manipulation by parents is deeply conditioned in our culture. Whether it manifests through verbal or non-verbal messages, guilt, or even by physical means, punishment renders children helpless. It sets in motion the squirrel cage, where children become trapped in a state of *able/unable*, which will ultimately drive all future behaviours.

If we want children to be free of this internal authority and be able to live deeply content with themselves, then we must watch our behaviour. If we want the world to be a more peaceful, caring place, then we need to spend time with our own children.

As I stood in front of my daughter as she bounced on the bed, the most important thing I could do was observe my behaviour and not react. This was important for her and her future, as well as mine — indeed, for the whole of humanity, too.

I make this bold claim not because it is easy. Observing your centralised mind is not sitting in a quiet room or on the beach meditating or performing a bendy manoeuvre on a rock for your Instagram account. Those are like shadowboxing when compared to an actual MMA cage fight.

Watching yourself parent is the hardest work you will ever undertake. Sitting in a cave meditating for years may seem arduous, but it's nothing compared to living with your children. Through this journey, we learn about ourselves — our inner nature. We see what's actually in the self in relation to others. It's akin to discovering your true fighting skills by stepping into a cage, not by merely shadowboxing or aikido. Parenting is the crucible that reveals the essence of who we are and how we interact with the world around us.

Meditation, often misunderstood and misconstrued at its core, is about understanding the self. It involves shining a light into the depths of our inner darkness. When trapped within the prison of our centralised mind, clarity becomes elusive as we are entangled in our own narratives. The key to seeing the truth lies in transitioning from this centralised state to a decentralised mind, where we can impartially observe what truly unfolds within us. Though the concept may seem straightforward, its implementation is challenging. The mind does not want to let go. The allure of constant motion, the hamster wheel, is so very seductive, yet we can pierce its illusory draw when we move past it and into the decentralised mind.

My two young children are my greatest gifts. They know my every weakness, and through them, I often find myself facing my shadow side. It's not pretty.

The fruits of his challenging work are remarkable. My children are growing into individuals who hold their own authority, capable of communicating with adults as equals. They are to self-regulate their emotions without being suppressed through manipulation by us. Don't get me wrong, sometimes I am tempted to take the easier path, yielding to manipulation, but I take my children seriously and value their integrity. In committing to fostering their autonomy and growth, I witness the emergence of empowered young souls who are navigating their way with resilience and self-awareness.

As I embraced my enhanced role as a parent, I discarded the weight and conditioning of traditional "fatherhood." Through observation, I discovered that the conventional parenting model was misaligned with my true desires. It became evident that adhering to those norms disrupted the deep love and connection I share with my children.

I have also begun questioning the practice of ubiquitous praise and encouragement, particularly the common British habit of using phrases like "good girl" or "good boy" when responding to children.

If you are unaware of this, next time you're in a playground or around parents, especially Brits, listen for this insidious conditioning cycle. "Oh, you're such a good girl," seems innocuous at a playground, but I grimace when I hear it. My wife even wants to print a t-shirt that reads, "Please don't 'good girl' my child as she is not a dog." The message to our children is clear: if you do a task well, you are a good girl/boy. But, if you make a mistake, which is an inevitable part of learning, an inner voice will remind you that you are a "bad girl" or "bad boy".

The negative conditioning is strikingly apparent, but only a few individuals step back and observe their own behaviour. Consequently, generations of damaging conditioning perpetuates itself. Parents, with the best intentions of raising capable children unknowingly influence them in the opposite direction. Because of their own conditioning, they know no other way.

To compound the problem, we send children into an educational system that fails to meet their needs. First, traditional education is structured around a set curriculum that children are required to master despite the fact that it may not match their interests. In the classroom, they are programmed to compete against each other for gold stars and grades, shallow rewards readily available to those children who understand that memorisation leads to praise and accolades. Not only is centralised education misguided, but it further reinforces a sense of helplessness in children who are uninterested in a predetermined set of subjects or who are unwilling to participate in the accolades-for-trained-tricks educational scheme.

Children are also compelled to spend time with peers they do not always like. Bullying can be profoundly damaging. Some adults argue that this breeds strong children and fosters ability, but it's likely these same adults experienced bullying and coercion from their own parents.

Once you grasp how children learn by being sponges to their environment, the idea of segregating them by age appears absurd as it retards their learning. Children flourish when they spend time interacting with different age groups. Indeed, a friend who works in education spent time with Lima and her self-directed learning friend, and he remarked that he had never seen more self-sufficient children.

Most parents must work all day to make ends meet, and I speak to many who are searching for alternatives to the traditional educational system. That so many parents feel drawn to changing their children's educational opportunities yet are forced to work excessive hours highlights how the modern monetary system has warped the value of money. Inflation has eroded our earnings to such an extent that people have to work increasingly longer hours just to stay afloat financially.

Transitioning to a bitcoin standard, which removes the state from our monetary system, will allow us to break free from this enslavement model, allowing humans to flourish once again. Likewise, removing state control from education will produce an educational renaissance, but that topic warrants exploration in another book.

Our family is very fortunate that my wife takes seriously the idea of children having freedom and sovereignty. On most days, we engage in discussions on this subject and hold each other accountable when we slip into old conditioning.

This transformative approach to parenting has opened our eyes to novel ways of nurturing our children. Inspired by the positive outcomes we've witnessed, we've decided to create a centre for parents and children. The centre will serve children, focusing on self-direct learning, which is my wife's passion. My role will be to teach parents how to free themselves from the tyranny of their own damaged conditioning.

Interestingly, as we develop this centre, we find the process brings to the surface triggering behaviours between us, both as a couple and as parents. Just this morning, I felt worried about the timely completion of the business plan, which is under my wife's purview. To quell my unease (a desire to feel less *unable* and more *able*), I mentioned it again to her. With a playful grin, I confessed I was sort of helicoptering her project. She reacted angrily to my inquiry. But, five years ago, this kind of situation would have led to an explosive argument, and my wife would have walked away, relying on the "flight" coping mechanism to assert her *able-ness*. Why? Because I triggered her *unable-ness* by asking about the project. My question came from an energy of able/unable, and it triggered the same in her.

By the way, we always choose partners with similar behavioural conditioning — always.

This time, however, I watched my behaviour. Unfortunately, I hadn't caught in time the initial triggering of *unable*, which led to the question, but I was aware now. My wife attacked me on another perceived wrongdoing, resorting to a straw man argumentation fallacy. Normally, this would have caused me to become confused, further increasing my unable-ness. This is why people invoke the straw man fallacy to advocate for themselves. (The straw man fallacy is when someone creates a false or distorted version of their opponent's argument and then attacks that false version.) Or, more simply said, when people feel *unable*, they take action to feel *able*. In this instance, the straw man fallacy was the most expedient route.

We discussed the intricacies of the straw man fallacy and calmed this interaction by acknowledging that both our behaviours had been triggered by conditioning. And, since I initiated the query about the business plan, I apologised. I emphasised the significance of carefully examining and understanding the underlying reasons for defensive emotions when they arise between us as a couple. This practice is essential for a strong relationship. Even so, the most important reason for discussing and observing our behaviour is that we are conditioning our two girls for their future relationships. If we shout and bicker, they will choose partners who also exhibit that behaviour. This cycle is inevitable.

As I advise clients, the mediation work, which is simply understanding the self, is like gold mining. We become enriched with gold, or even better — bitcoin, by sifting through the debris kicked up by our conditioning. Achieving freedom is like Sirius Black's escape from Azkaban in the Harry Potter series. (Excuse the Potter reference; I am deep in the Potter saga with my daughter, so I need to throw in a storyline as a tribute.)

So after a lull, with a slight grin, I asked my wife how long she planned to distance herself from me — a whole day like her mother or a year like her father. Relieved by the levity, she smiled, and we hugged. We humans behave the way we do because we get something — positive or negative — from it. When our conditioning flares, it is like a drug to bathe in, an addictive self-righteousness, but it makes our lives hell on earth. Such corrosive behaviour is damaging not only to all our relationships but also to us internally, damaging our cells and systems.

To this end, I have begun working more with parents, coaching them to see the patterns of their own limiting conditioning so that they, too, can walk the beautiful journey of self-discovery — for their children and for themselves.

We have great aspirations for the centre we are creating together. It will be designed as a place where kids can flourish, empowered by the freedom to choose what they want to learn and to pursue their curiosities. Beyond that, we aim to ignite a sense of wonder and inspiration in parents, guiding them to explore the beauty of life without the weight of conditioning inherited from their ancestors and the collective society.

If parents want children who are *able*, they must first look at their own deep *unable-ness*. This is the secret to happy kids who enjoy their lives.

> *"To trust children we must first learn to trust ourselves... and most of us were taught as children that we could not be trusted".*
>
> — John Holt

7

Becoming Masterless

At present, we have witnessed the successful emergence of decentralised money facilitated by the invention of a decentralised internet, which has further decentralised information. It is thus natural and logical to imagine that decentralisation will occur elsewhere. In fact, it may be a governing feature of our fabric of reality. Let's first look at the improvements offered by shifting from centralised and conditioned psychology toward a decentralised mind.

A centralised mind operates on perception, relying on a system of duality and comparison to make sense of reality. A notable flow with this system is that whenever we seek to manifest or shape our reality, it inadvertently energises the opposite, as well. The solution to this glitch lies in embracing a decentralised mind, where such limitations and contradictions can be resolved.

Decentralised Health

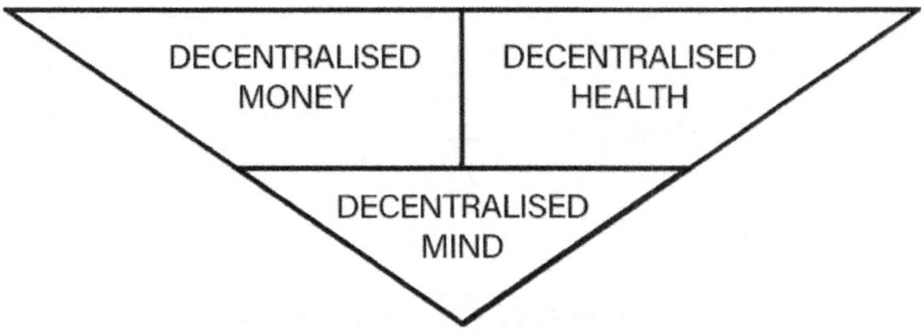

The Decentralised System

Picture a future where decentralised money forms the bedrock of the economy. Societal norms will now rest upon truth, mathematics, and an inability to print free money with corrupt value. Humans will finally be able to transact based on fair value, giving rise to a genuinely free market.

In such a world, decentralised health will steer us away from a centralised, controlling authority like the pharmaceutical industry toward a balanced, holistic approach — a radical shift from disease care to wellness care, which has completely captured and corrupted our healthcare system, has in fact become a disease care system.

Having been captured and corrupted by Big Pharma, Big Medicine, and loose money, our current healthcare system is based on medicating symptoms, leading to a growing demand for specialised treatments for each individual illness, neglecting the root cause of the problem. Embracing a decentralized health model entails adopting a holistic approach to our bodies. This approach bears a striking resemblance to traditional Chinese medicine, where we consider the human as a whole, taking into account factors like sleep, the individual's environment, diet, and the information and entertainment they consume. By looking at the bigger picture, we can gain a deeper understanding of our health and well-being.

The practice of restoring balance to the body is not a new concept; other cultures have integrated this concept for millennia. Our scientific community is gradually shifting towards a similar understanding, but the pursuit of truth is hindered by the for-profit medical industry and Big Pharma. Interestingly, the world's preeminent mitochondrial researcher has established an institute in China, speculating that the meridian lines in acupuncture could potentially serve as the electrical signalling pathways of mitochondria.

Years ago, I watched an acupuncturist, whom I am still friends with today, treat a player at Chelsea FC. Despite achieving remarkable results, the team physiotherapists scoffed at his methods, calling it woo-woo and magic. These days, physiotherapy routinely incorporates acupuncture. The classic phrase "First they laugh at you, then they fight you, then they join you." seems apt here.

Pain and disease in the body are akin to the oil light in the car blinking, signalling that an oil change is required. Our current healthcare model places duct tape over the light because we believe the flashing light is the issue. In essence, we overlook the underlying cause and focus solely on suppressing the symptoms, again neglecting the root issue.

> *"The doctor of the future will give no medicine, but will instruct his patients in the care of the human frame, in diet, and in the cause and prevention of disease."*
>
> — Thomas Edison

In contrast, decentralised health empowers individuals to comprehend the fundamental requirements of their bodies, all of which are freely accessible, granting them sovereignty over their health and well-being.

Once again, self-authority to be masterless.

Based on research and years of observation, I propose a shift toward a decentralised health system. This system is free and accessible to all, and it requires you to understand that the body functions as an electrical system.

Your Electrical system

The first part of the health paradigm shift would be seeing the body as an electrical system. This has been known for centuries. In the past, the whole Chinese medical system was based on the idea of chi: this energy that flows through the body and whenever that flows freely without blockage, then there is no illness or imbalance. But when this becomes stagnated and blocked, you will start to see inflammation, infections, and diseases appear. Traditional Chinese medicine, or TCM for short, is based on Taoist principles of watching nature to learn about our internal ecosystem.

Whenever there is a blocked river, parasites and pathogens start to take hold. When you remove the block from the river, that will instantly clear the infestation. The Western approach in this scenario would be the use of pesticides to exterminate the bugs, and that will need to be repeated continuously as the block is still there.

Trying to kill each one and spray them can initially help, but that comes with its own side effects as well as toxicity and poisoning of the environment in the long term. This is analogous to the overprescription of drugs we see today.

So, by removing the block or the root cause, the river will rebalance itself. We can apply the same idea to the body by finding the root cause of the blockage or the block so that the body can rebalance itself. The skill lies in finding where the block is, and we can use Mediation OS and energetics to do that.

The Chinese understood that how a person thinks and behaves, his environment, and his emotional state by thinking or through fears suppressed in the body slows down the movement of energy. So, emotions have an effect on the body. Now, you can see from pain, research, and pain science that our perception and our emotions affect our body. There is much more research in Western medicine needed in this area, as the paradigm is still one of a mechanical body with the mind as something separate.

So we have to be able to clear energy that gets stuck in our body. This can be done by doing simple Qigong exercises, self-massage, or lightning meditation.

The central mind weakens our internal battery. When we move to a decentralised mind, we can limit this effect. So, my model of decentralised health comes with the decentralised mind and the idea that we need to be observed to resolve our own emotions. We have to be able to work with ourselves like our own computer to resolve all the emotions and things so that it does not come in and slow down the meridians of the body. This is very simple to do once you know how.

Most of the miraculous results I have had with clients were simply from removing the emotions that were impeding the flow of energy in the body. Again, this may sound very woo-woo to some, and it is what I used to think, but almost three decades later, I see this as the truth. It seems that Western science is moving closer to this truth, which is inevitable.

The next aspect of decentralised health is charging our internal battery with external sources.

Charging Your Battery

Douglas Wallace, a renowned 50-year-old leading researcher in the field of mitochondria — the body's energy system — posits that approximately 85% of chronic disease can be attributed to mitochondrial dysfunction. He asserts that mitochondrial health is pivotal to the body's health and wellness.

Why are mitochondria important?

Mitochondria dysfunction has skyrocketed in the last 70 years while, at the same time, time spent outside has decreased dramatically over the past century.

The mitochondrial system is activated and stimulated by light via receptors in the body. Basking in sunlight or spending time in nature, which reflects infrared light, produces deep healing properties for the body, bolstering and stimulating the body's electrical system.

More specifically, the sun's rays are a charging source for our batteries. And the best part is that it costs nothing to step outside and enjoy nature. Studies have substantiated that being in nature improves our immune system and decreases inflammation. As in a normal battery that must stay fully charged, our bodies require proper hydration. In fact, inside our cells, the mitochondria create their own water via reverse photosynthesis. The combination of light, water, and electromagnetic fields forms the battery that is critical for our health. Reconnecting with the Earth can be as simple as drinking water and removing our shoes. Sadly, even wearing shoes isolates us from the Earth, deepening our disconnect from nature. Yet, it costs nothing to kick off our shoes and "touch grass" as they say.

The healing power of the sun and its use in medical treatment like heliotherapy have roots extending back into antiquity. However, with the discovery of antibiotics, the focus shifted towards drug treatments for diseases like tuberculosis in the 1950s, and heliotherapy gradually fell out of favour, becoming almost forgotten. The advent of antibiotics brought about efficiency by reducing expenses and minimising disruptions to individual lives, resulting in lower hospitalisation rates in some cases. We must also remember that heliotherapy's efficacy in harnessing the sun's healing power remains a remarkable and timeless aspect of health and wellness.[1]

[1]Baggerly CA et al. *Sunlight and Vitamin D: Necessary for Public Health*. J Am Coll Nutr. 2015;34(4):359-65. doi: 10.1080/07315724.2015.1039866. Epub 2015 Jun 22. PMID: 26098394; PMCID: PMC4536937.

In my own pursuit of health, I sought to live in a place with abundant sunlight throughout the year. After careful consideration, we chose a location not too far from my parents, Madeira, Portugal.

Once settled, my wife and I rose before sunrise to watch the sun crest the horizon. We watched until the sun became too intense to gaze at directly. Within a few days, my sleep at night improved dramatically, and I found myself going to bed earlier, around 9 pm, and sleeping through until 6:30 – 7 am.

While I cannot pinpoint the exact cause of the change in my sleep patterns, the results were undeniably positive. My energy level throughout the day was constant, and I no longer took a power nap after lunch, which had become a routine necessity for me if I wanted to function adequately later in the day.

Researchers in a recent sleep study found that people who were exposed to greater amounts of light during the morning hours, between 8 am and Noon, fell asleep more quickly at night and had fewer sleep disturbances during the night compared to those exposed to low light in the morning.[2]

Daily sunlight should be a prescription for each of us. Although it can be difficult in the UK and other Northern countries to access ample sunlight, technology has opened up possibilities for us to solve this issue using red light therapy. We simply need the right research and data on how we can best maintain our health.

---

[2]Figueiro MG et al. *The impact of daytime light exposures on sleep and mood in office workers.* Sleep Health. 2017 Jun;3(3):204-215. doi: 10.1016/j.sleh.2017.03.005. Epub 2017 Apr 23. PMID: 28526259.

In addition to adequate sunlight exposure, we need to move every day and fuel our bodies with whole, natural foods that come directly from nature. And since our soil is depleted, adding a pinch of natural salt to our water is a good idea. Rest and high-quality sleep are vital to the recovery and rejuvenation of both our mind and body. Sleep, in particular, is a magical gift to us, and remarkably, it is free. Yet, the prevalence of screen usage, as we seek distraction from the entrapment of the centralised mind, poses a great challenge to the health of humanity. The blue light emitted by screens can disrupt our sleep. Thus, we must regulate our desire for distraction and shift our focus to the decentralised mind.

I have meticulously focused on finding a system that would keep me in optimal shape, both physically and mentally, that would be self-sustaining. Now, I want to show you how to access this skill-set.

It is free and accessible to all and consists of three main factors:

1. Understanding your body functions as an electrical system;
2. charging your internal battery with external sources; and
3. finding and removing weakening programs and the weak points they create.

I hope you enjoy finding these truths within yourself, and I look forward to witnessing more humans living a decentralised, fully optimised life.

★★★

Acknowledgements

A massive thank you to Niko, Mel and Konsensus Network for helping me with this book. Absolutely invaluable work to shape and help create it. Appreciate you!

I also want to thank everyone who I've encountered in my life. I have learnt from every one of you, some enjoyable, and some not, depending on my programming. Life is an internal adventure game, and everyone I met showed me something I still needed to discover. Here's to discovering more levels so I can experience life fully.

★★★★★

NY

About the Author

Rob Brinded stands at the forefront of mind-body medicine, dedicating decades to unravelling the intricate links between our mental and physical well-being. His extensive experience collaborating with elite athletes has enriched his insights into the symbiotic relationship between the mind and the body.

Currently, alongside his family in Madeira, Rob supports his wife, Sylvia, pioneering an UnSchooling initiative, A Place To Be Be, whilst continuing his online clinic and writing his new book on *The Hamster Wheels of the Mind*. In his leisure, he passionately shares insights on bitcoin, subtly orange-pilling local eateries, masseurs, and barber shops.

https://twitter.com/RobBrinded

Send bitcoin to Rob.

Printed in Dunstable, United Kingdom

64372772R00068